D I S C O V E R
Birds

Contributing writer:
Scott Weidensaul

Consultant:
Todd A. Culver

Publications International, Ltd.

Louis Weber, C.E.O.
Publications International, Ltd.
7373 North Cicero Avenue
Lincolnwood, Illinois 60646

Permission is never granted for commercial purposes.

Manufactured in Yugoslavia.

8 7 6 5 4 3 2 1

ISBN:
1-56173-108-0

Photo credits:

Front cover: Clayton A. Fogle; Superstock; O.S. Pettingill/VIREO
Back cover: C.H. Greenewalt/VIREO

Animals Animals: Doug Allan: 34; Donn Renn: 35; Charles &
Elizabeth Schwartz: 8; **Kent & Donna Dannen:** Table of contents;
Clayton A. Fogle: 4, 8, 9, 19, 23, 24, 36, 42–44, back endsheet; **FPG
International:** Front endsheet, 14, 40; Gary Brownell: Back endsheet;
H. Lanks: Front endsheet; Bill Losh: Front endsheet, 18; 40; Len Rue,
Jr.: 17; Schmidt: 25; L. West: Front endsheet; **Images of Nature:**
Thomas D. Mangelsen: 10, 12, 30, 33; **Steven C. Kaufman:** 12, 30,
32, 33, back endsheet; **R.Y. Kaufman/Yogi:** 13, 26, 32, 33, back
endsheet; **Stan Osolinski:** 26; **Photri:** Lani Howe: Front endsheet,
table of contents; B. Kulik: 18, 20; M. Long: 22; Leonard Lee Rue III:
21, 23, 28, 37. **Superstock:** 11; **Tom Stack & Associates
Photographers:** Mary Clay: 23; Thomas Kitchin: 15, 18; Brian
Parker: Front endsheet; Don & Esther Phillips: 28; Robert Rozinski/
Wend Shattil: Table of contents; Kevin Schafer: 39; Dave Watts: 31;
VIREO: S. Bahrt: 4, 34, 35; A. Carey: 7, 12, 28; Allan & Helen
Cruickshank: 10, 11, 17, 20, 21, 23; J. Dunning: 36, 39, 40; Sam Fried:
10; W. Greene: 27; C.H. Greenewalt: Front endsheet, title page, table
of contents, 6, 16, back endsheet; B. Henry: 6, 24, 30; B.M. Jett: 38;
Lou Jost: 40; M.P. Kahl: 22; S.J. Lang: 4, 5, 18; A. Morris: Front
endsheet, 14, 16, 20, back endsheet; C. Munn: 43; J.P. Myers: 32;
J. Oakley: 29; O.S. Pettingill: 35; R. Ridgely: 42; D. Roby: 35, back
endsheet; F.K. Schleicher: 4; B. Schorre: 11, 24, 27; Ned Smith: 6, 17;
F.S. Todd: 34; D. Wechsler: 36, 38, 41; B.K. Wheeler: 15, 29;
J.R. Woodward: 14, 16; **Kathy Watkins:** 15.

Scott Weidensaul
Contributing writer

Contributing writer Scott Weidensaul is a freelance writer specializing
in natural history books. He is also a wildlife artist whose work has
been the focus of a number of exhibits including a show sponsored by
the National Wildlife Federation.

Todd A. Culver
Consultant

Consultant Todd A. Culver is the Education Specialist at Cornell
Laboratory of Ornithology at Cornell University. He contributes to the
nationally aired radio program *Birdwatch*.

Illustrations: Pablo Montes O'Neill; Lorie Robare Discover Birds

CONTENTS

IN YOUR BACKYARD,

you'll find birds that do not mind sharing their world with humans. Whether you have a city plot, a suburban yard, or a quiet farm,

there are dozens and dozens of birds that build their nests and raise their young in the presence of people.

Backyard birds come in all shapes and sizes, from the tiny hummingbird to the bright blue jay. They eat nuts, seeds, berries, fruit, and insects. They will welcome wintertime sprinklings of seeds in the snow. Planting berry bushes and fruit trees are inviting, too.

Watching for tracks on the ground or in the snow will tell you who has been visiting your backyard. It may have been a wren, robin, oriole, or jay. Take a moment and enjoy the show.

THE CARDINAL

The dull color of the female cardinal helps to hide her as she sits on her eggs. Young cardinals are dark and have little or no red.

When building the nest, the female often stops to sit in it and shape it to her body.

The male cardinal is the only crested red bird in North America. It is red all over except for its black face and throat. The male cardinal is about eight inches long, beak to tail. The female cardinal has her mate's shape, including the crest that she can raise or lower as her mood changes. Her colors are much softer, though—brownish-pink, with a tinge of red on her crest, wings, and tail.

The cardinal's favorite food is black-oil sunflower seeds. When eating a sunflower seed, the cardinal uses its tongue to position the seed sideways in its bill. The cardinal cracks the seed open, spits out the hull, and swallows the nut meat. Cardinals also like to eat insects, pumpkin seeds, grains, and fruit.

In the days of the settlers, cardinals lived only in the southeastern states. Over the last 200 years, as forests have been cleared to make room for towns and farms, the habitat for cardinals has improved. Cardinals are now found in the northern states and in southern Canada.

Cardinals do not like deep wooded places. They prefer the forest's edge, suburban gardens, groves, and parks. Above the chatter of squirrels and scolding of jays, you may hear the cardinal's *who-it, who-it, who-it, cheer cheer cheer!*

The cardinal's heavy beak is especially suited for cracking hard seeds.

AMERICAN ROBIN

The red breast of the robin not only makes it easy for people to identify, it is also the way other robins recognize each other. The male's breast is brighter than the female's; their young have speckled breasts.

Robins build their nest of twigs, grass, and mud. The nest is plastered to a tree branch, deep in a bush, or on a windowsill or another flat place. The female usually lays four pale blue eggs.

from here to here in summer

from here to here in winter

MIGRATORY MAP

In winter, most robins migrate in flocks to the warm south-central states. Some robins will stay north, though, so you may see robins in your snowy yard. When their inner clocks tell them winter is over, the migrating males will flock back to their nesting grounds first. The females and yearlings will follow in the next few weeks.

Robins eat whatever is plentiful during the season. In winter, they will eat mostly vegetables, fruits, and berries. In summer, they eat mostly insects.

One of the first signs that spring is on its way is the red-breasted robin singing outside your window!

Can a robin hear a worm wiggling through soil? Ornithologists don't think so. Because its eyes are on the sides of its head, a robin must cock its head sideways to see its food.

HUMMINGBIRDS

Hummingbirds have long, needle-like bills, which they use to sip nectar from flowers. Their feet are small and weak. They may be terrific aviators, but they can barely walk, and hardly ever do.

The acrobatics of hummingbirds help them to defend their territories, attract mates, and scare other birds.

Hummingbirds have extremely powerful flight muscles. In most birds, only the muscles that control the downstroke of wing motion are enlarged. In the hummingbird both the muscles that control the upstroke as well as those that control the downstroke are powerful. In flight, a hummingbird beats its wings 55 to 75 times a second!

Hummingbirds are the smallest birds in the world. This black-chinned hummingbird measures 3 to 4 inches from bill to tail.

Since the hummingbird is the smallest bird in the world, it naturally builds the smallest nest.

Hummingbirds can fly in every direction, including upside down! While they hover, their wings rotate at the shoulder; their tips trace a figure-8 pattern. Darting and dipping at a high speed is their best survival technique. Nothing can catch them!

Most North American species of hummingbirds produce two broods per season. Egg color varies according to the species, but many eggs look pinkish to white. The eggs are oval, and are less than one half-inch long. The female incubates the eggs from 11 to 19 days. The ruby-throated hummingbird egg hatches in 11 to 14 days.

The hummingbird's favorite color is red. Scientists believe that hummingbirds are not born with this preference, but learn it through trial and error. Hummingbirds discover that red flowers provide a source of nectar with the amount of sugar they prefer. To invite hummingbirds to your yard, hang a special red feeder that holds a sugar-water syrup made of one part table sugar and four parts water. Do not use honey and water. It spoils quickly and can poison the little birds.

When hummingbirds sip nectar from flowers, they become dusted with pollen. Just as bees do, hummingbirds help to cross-pollinate flowers. In fact, some flowers rely on hummingbirds rather than bees for pollination.

Hummingbirds must eat enormous amounts of food to fuel themselves. Nectar is an easily digested source of quick energy. It is thought that a hummingbird eats half its weight in sugar each day. It collects the nectar by drawing its tongue in and out of the flower about 13 times a second.

Many species of hummingbirds have a narrow crop below the throat. The crop is a place to store food that is gathered but cannot be swallowed and digested at the moment.

The nest of a ruby-throated hummingbird is only as big around as a half-dollar; the eggs are smaller than a dime! The nest stretches as the babies inside it grow. Some hummingbirds use the same nest year after year.

BLUE JAY

At a feeder, blue jays show a liking for sunflower seeds, but their favorite food is peanuts! Jays will crack open whole nuts if they must.

If a jay finds more food than it can eat, it will "cache" it in a dead tree or in a hole in the ground.

The blue jay is a member of the crow family. Like its relatives, there is no difference in color or patterns between the males and females.

Not everyone is happy to see a blue jay in their yard. Many people enjoy the jay's brightness and boldness. Other people do not like the jay because it seems to be a mean bird. It often chases smaller birds away from the feeder. And it is known for stealing eggs and chicks, which it eats, from the nests of other birds.

No wild animal is "good" or "bad." The blue jay simply lives its life as it is supposed to. It does sometimes prey on the eggs and babies of songbirds, but most of the time it eats insects, worms, seeds, fruit, berries, and acorns.

Jays will choose to nest in a pine rather than a leafy tree. The thick pine tree will hide the nest and help keep the nestlings safe. The male and female build their nest together. But the male does not share the job of incubating the eggs. He brings food to his mate while she sits on the eggs. When the chicks have hatched, the male and female will both care for them. The family will stay together through the summer and sometimes into the winter. When winter comes, they join a larger flock.

Unlike most backyard birds, the blue jay does not migrate. Only jays that live in the far north—in Canada and New England—will fly south for the winter. Even then, they fly south only until the winter is a little milder.

ORIOLE

Not all birds make nests. Some simply scrape a shallow dip in the ground; some lay their eggs on bare cliff ledges. But the oriole's nest is a marvel. It is a carefully woven sack of grass and plant stems that hangs down from a high branch, protecting the eggs and chicks inside a soft pocket. It may look flimsy, but it is really very strong. It is able to withstand strong winds and driving rain.

The female oriole builds the nest, though her mate may help. First, she picks the right branch, usually one that is at least 25 to 30 feet from the ground. Orioles have been known to build their nests as much as 80 feet high. The best branch is slim and droopy, so a raccoon or other enemy would not want to crawl out on it.

The female oriole starts to build her nest by looping strands of grass, plant fibers, or string around a fork in the branch. Once this base has been woven, she collects much longer pieces of material, often stripping the tough fibers from stalks of weeds like milkweed. These long strands form the sides and bottom of the pouch; hundreds of pieces are needed to finish the nest. It may take her two weeks to finish the nest if materials are hard to find.

In the summer, orioles are found all over the United States—except in the deep south.

You can "help" the busy female oriole build her nest by hanging pieces of yarn on tree branches and bushes where the oriole may find them.

Orioles in the east and west are so different they were considered separate species for many years. In the east they are called "Baltimore orioles" and in the west they are called "Bullock's orioles."

11

OVER FARMS AND FIELDS

are birds that do not like deep wilderness. Many birds prefer to live in open fields scattered with small woodlots and brushy fencerows. These are the birds of the farmlands.

Farm and field birds are among the most familiar, since they live so close to humans. They are often the easiest birds to watch. Walking along a country road in summer, you will probably see swallows chasing insects through the air, diving and swooping across the sky. There will be flocks of crows sitting on branches or telephone wires, nervously calling *caw! caw!* if they sense danger nearby. Pheasant or quail peek from the grasses along the road; sparrows of all sorts flit among the weeds. And high in the sky, a red-tailed hawk soars easily on the warm breeze.

AMERICAN CROW

The crow has an "all-purpose" bill. It is strong, sharp, and long—perfect for eating whatever food the crow can find.

When the farmer plows his fields, the crows will follow the tractor—at a safe distance—picking up the worms, insects, and mice that the plow uncovers. When the corn in that field sprouts, crows will pull up some of the shoots and eat them. They also eat many pesty insects, though, making up for the crops they destroy.

People who study them think crows are one of the smartest birds in the world. Crows have learned to eat grain that has fallen in the fields; they pick through dumps and garbage cans for scraps of food; and they pick at road-killed animals without getting killed by a car themselves.

Crows live in flocks most of the year. As many as 200,000 crows may roost together in one flock! During the breeding season, pairs go off by themselves to build their large stick nests.

The American crow usually lays four to six eggs. Both male and female incubate the eggs for 18 days. The chicks leave the nest in 28 to 35 days. A pair of crows may nest a second time if their first nesting fails for any reason.

Crows are nature's garbage-collectors!

RED-TAILED HAWK

The adult red-tailed hawk's rusty tail is its best field mark, but don't expect to always see it. The orange-red color is only on top of the tail; it is invisible when you are looking up at a soaring hawk. Only if a circling hawk tilts to one side will you catch a glimpse of this marking.

High above the ground, the red-tailed hawk watches carefully for movement below. Like all hawks, its eyes are much better than ours at picking out details. A hawk that is hundreds of feet in the air can spot a mouse running through the grass. The red-tailed hawk's diet changes with the seasons, eating what is most abundant at that time. They mostly eat small mammals, like mice, shrews, voles, rabbits, and chipmunks. As with most predators, they will catch whatever they can, and their diet sometimes includes other birds, snakes, frogs, lizards, and large insects.

The undersides of the hawk are white. Seen from below, the tail looks slightly pink, especially if the sun is shining through it.

Even though red-tailed hawks hunt over open country, they nest in trees. They build large stick nests high in the branches.

Compared to smaller birds, hawks do not lay many eggs. The normal clutch for a red-tailed hawk is just two or three eggs. The chicks are unable to move at birth, but are not as helpless as songbird babies, for they have their eyes open and are covered with soft down. In a few days, they beg their parents for food. They are growing fast!

The red-tailed hawk eats live prey. Its bill is sharp and curved for shredding pieces of meat.

BARN SWALLOW

Swallows feed on almost nothing but insects they snatch out of mid-air. They even drink while flying!

The barn swallow's tail is long and forked. It is the only swallow in North America with such a tail.

Mud balls are the building blocks of a barn-swallow nest. Both male and female barn swallows gather at mud puddles to scoop up mud that's just right—not too dry, not too wet. The swallows shape the mud into small blobs and carry them in their bills back to their nesting sites. Layer upon layer of mud balls are plastered on a barn rafter, or other wide beam, to create a half-circle of mud, mixed with weeds, grass, and plant roots. As the finishing touch, the nest is lined with feathers, especially white ones.

Barn swallows are common in farmland and open country over most of the United States and Canada. They are one of the easiest birds to identify: Both male and female are dark, glossy blue, with a cinnamon-colored breast and a rusty-brown throat. A young barn swallow looks much like the adult barn swallow, but its tail may be less forked. They are also much paler and duller in color.

Swallows eat insects they catch in mid-air. Several days of chilly rain can mean disaster for swallows, since few insects fly in such weather. This kind of weather is especially bad if it happens during the nesting season. During this time, parents must feed their chicks as well as themselves.

A swallow carrying a fluffy chicken feather back to its nest may have to fight off its neighbors, who will try to steal the prize.

RING-NECKED PHEASANT

By far, the most colorful farmland bird is the male ring-necked pheasant with his green head, red face, white collar, and long tail.

Even though they are strong in flight, pheasants spend most of their time on the ground. They are able to run quickly if they are in danger. Even a brightly colored male can vanish like magic; his many colors actually break up his outline and help to hide him.

In spring, the plain brown females nest in grass pastures and hay fields, where the plants will hide her. She makes a grass nest on the ground and lays as many as 15 pale brown eggs. The chicks hatch in 23 to 25 days. Once her chicks have hatched, the hen leads them to grain fields where they will find plenty of insects to eat. Even though adult pheasants eat seeds, the chicks must have insects, which are high in protein and good for growing bodies.

Pheasants live mostly in brushy fencerows, overgrown fields, and weed-choked gullies.

In winter, many of the fields will have been cut and plowed under. The pheasant flocks may move to frozen cattail swamps or wooded thickets for cover, only coming out to feed. They will eat corn and other grains that farmers have left on the ground, as well as weed seeds, sumac berries, fallen apples, and whatever other plant food they can find.

The pale brown color of the pheasant's eggs helps to hide them in their grassy nest on the ground.

Pheasant chicks can walk and run just a few hours after they hatch. But if danger approaches, they know to stand perfectly still. They seem to disappear!

17

At THE WATER'S EDGE

is one of the best places to look for birds—or for any

kind of wildlife, really. It might be along the seashore, at the border of a marsh, or near a pond in a park.

Much of the reason why birds are plentiful near water is that food is easy to find there. The water's edge has a lot to offer a hungry bird. There are plants for grazers, and small prey for hunters, like herons and egrets. Some birds, like gulls, feed on a wide variety of food, including scraps left by humans.

Birds that live along the water have special features that help them survive. Oily feathers keep ducks warm and dry. Long legs keep herons and flamingos from getting wet.

18

GULLS

The laughing gull is named for its strange call.

Gulls are scavengers, eating whatever they happen to find —even an unattended picnic!

Ring-billed gulls are found on both fresh and salt water over much of North America.

Some types of gulls learned to carry clams and mussels high in the air and drop them onto rocks or even roads, cracking them open.

There are herring gulls and ring-billed gulls, laughing gulls and black-backed gulls. There are more than two dozen different kinds of gulls in North America! But there's one gull you'll never find—the "sea gull." There is no such bird by that name! In fact, gulls are often found hundreds of miles from the ocean. We should remember to call them by their correct name, just plain "gulls."

The herring gull is big and noisy. It is found over almost all of the northern hemisphere, though it is rare in desert lands of the American west. Herring gulls are about two feet long, bill to tail, with a wing-span of about four and one half feet.

At first glance, ring-billed gulls look very much like herring gulls, but they are smaller and slimmer. The adults have yellow legs and a yellow bill with a dark band near its tip (that's how it got its name).

In the spring and summer, the laughing gull sports a dark black head and red bill. When the breeding season is over, this gull molts so that its head turns white with a touch of gray around the back. The bill changes to black. Laughing gulls are almost always found near salt water.

The famous pouch of the pelican, which the old rhyme says "can hold more than its belly can," is used for catching fish. Here's how it works: The pelican flies low over the water, just a few yards above the surface. When it sees a fish that is not too deep, the pelican dives down and throws its wings back, hitting the water beak-first. The pelican opens its beak as it hits the water. The pouch balloons out and "nets" the fish. When the pelican bobs back to the surface of the water, it points its bill down and forces the water out of its pouch. The pelican tips its head back and swallows the fish.

The brown pelican's nest may be built on the ground, on cliffs, or in trees, but it will always be part of a pelican colony. A pelican colony may be part of an even larger colony of pelicans, cormorants, egrets, and herons. In the 1960s and 1970s the number of brown pelicans took a dangerous drop. Insecticides, especially DDT, were poisoning coastal waters. The chemical DDT caused the pelican's eggshells to be so thin that the eggs broke when the female tried to sit on them. The brown pelican was named as an endangered species, but as the use of dangerous pesticides has stopped, the pelican is growing in numbers.

Young pelicans are born without feathers but soon are covered in gray down. They eat partly digested fish from the pouches of their parents.

Pelicans live in large, noisy flocks. They often live among other shore birds, like egrets and cormorants.

Scientists have found fossils that make them think pelicans have been around—unchanged—for 30 million years! That's much longer than man has been around.

21

FLAMINGOS

A flamingo's long legs and neck help it to feed without getting its body wet.

A flamingo chick drinks rich crop-milk, which is made in the parent's throat.

One place where flamingos do not live in the wild is Florida! The flamingos in Florida parks and zoos are captive birds.

The flamingo has become a symbol of the tropics, but there are really six different species of flamingos found all over the world. One kind of flamingo lives high in the snowy Andes Mountains!

Diet plays a big role in a flamingo's color. Captive flamingos must eat tiny shrimp to stay looking their best.

The flamingo's big, downward-hooked bill and long legs and neck help it to feed. The flamingo can wade in water without getting its body wet. Stretching its neck down and holding its head upside down, the flamingo dips its bill below the water and pumps water in and out. Filters in the mouth strain out tiny shellfish, bugs, and algae, which the flamingo swallows. In many ways, the flamingo's bill is upside down. The tongue is attached to the roof of the mouth. The upper part of the bill is the part that moves; the lower part is fixed to the skull. But when the flamingo feeds, its head is upside down, so the bill and tongue work "normally." Flamingos often feed in muddied water, but the dirty meal doesn't seem to harm the flamingo.

Flamingos nest in huge colonies, sometimes numbering hundreds of thousands of birds. The nest is a large cup built of mud on the ground. The nest holds a single egg.

MALLARD

When you think of a wild duck, you probably picture a mallard. With its green head, chestnut-brown chest, and orange feet, the male mallard—or "drake"—is one of the best-known birds in the world. It is no wonder: The mallard is found all over the northern hemisphere and in Africa.

Mallard drakes are unmistakable. But the females, called hens, are less colorful and may be confused with females of other species. The mallard hen is brown, with a pale head. Her bill is orange with a large black splotch. Her legs and feet are orange, too. The hen and drake both have large, shiny blue patches on their wings; the wing edges are striped with thin bars of black and white. No other puddle duck has this combination.

Mallards pair up in winter while snow is still on the ground. The hen does all the work of raising the chicks. She finds a quiet, hidden spot for the nest, sometimes very far from water. The nest itself is built on the ground. It is a shallow bowl of grass lined with feathers the hen plucks from her breast. The chicks hatch with a fluffy coat of down. Their eyes are open, and they can walk and feed themselves right away.

As soon as her chicks have hatched, the hen leads them to the water for their first swimming lesson.

Mallards belong to the group of birds known as puddle ducks. They prefer shallow ponds, marshes, and lakes.

23

DEEP IN THE FORESTS

of North America are birds that hardly ever see people. Living among the tall, leafy trees, these birds are shy and difficult to watch. The woodland bird's habitat—or neighborhood—

serves him well, though. It offers safe places for nests and plenty of insects to feed growing baby birds.

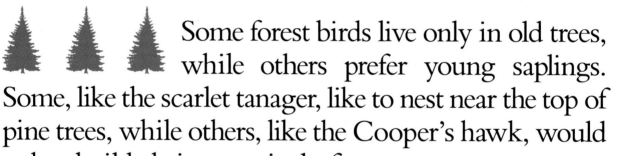

Some forest birds live only in old trees, while others prefer young saplings. Some, like the scarlet tanager, like to nest near the top of pine trees, while others, like the Cooper's hawk, would rather build their nests in leafy trees. Some birds can adapt to any kind of forest. Owls don't seem to care where they live. They can be found in all forests.

24

WOODPECKERS

There is hardly a forest in North America that does not have woodpeckers living among its trees.

This pair of woodpeckers will not only work on their nest hole together, they will raise their babies together, too.

A woodpecker's tail feathers are stiff and strong to help the bird brace itself while drilling.

A woodpecker is adapted to a life of striking hard things with its beak—something that other birds would find painful. But not the woodpecker! Its beak is specially built to make it strong. There is also a layer of padding at the base of its skull to absorb the shock of hammering.

The woodpecker has special feet, too. Its feet help the woodpecker to hang onto the side of a tree. Hanging there with its strong claws, the woodpecker leans back and braces its stiff tail feathers against the tree. Then, *b-r-r-r-r-r!* the woodpecker's drilling rings through the forest. Once it has carved a hole, the bird sticks its long, barbed, sticky tongue inside and plucks out insects, which it eats.

It is not surprising that woodpeckers nest in a hole carved in a tree. A new nest hole is made each spring, which may keep the number of insect pests low. The woodpeckers usually choose a branch that slopes up from the tree trunk, under which they cut a hole. This way, the nest hole will be protected from bad weather.

Males and females tend to hunt in different parts of a tree. The female will work along the trunk the male will drill higher in the tree or on smaller branches. With these "rules," it is easier for both woodpeckers to find enough to eat.

WOOD WARBLERS

The highlight of a birdwatcher's spring is the sight of a flock of warblers feeding in the treetops, hungry after a night of migrating. No other group of North American songbirds is as beautiful as these feathered gems.

There are more than 50 species of warblers found north of Mexico. Many more live in the tropics.

Warblers also nest in the treetops, so we know very little about their habits. We do know that the female lays about four eggs, which she incubates for 11 days. The females are usually drab, to help them hide while they are incubating their eggs.

There are fewer and fewer woodland songbirds these days—especially warblers and thrushes. Ornithologists think one problem is here in North America: By chopping down trees to make way for roads, power lines, and buildings, people have divided the forests into smaller and smaller pieces. Doing this allows predators that usually stay out of the deep woods—crows, blue jays, and raccoons—into the birds' breeding grounds.

Warbler males of most species are brightly marked in yellow, orange, red, green, or blue. The females are not as colorful, perhaps to help them hide while they incubate their eggs.

The warbler's beak is thin and sharp for catching insects.

Great horned owlets hatch at different times. If food is scarce, the oldest owlet will get it all. This way, at least one owlet will live instead of all of them starving to death.

On a frosty January night, the deep *whooo, whooo, whooo* of a pair of great horned owls fills the woods. Even though it is the middle of winter, the owls are beginning their courtship. By February they have chosen their nest, which will probably be an old one once belonging to hawks, squirrels, or crows. The nest may be the top of a broken tree. Either way, the female will add a little down to the nest lining. Otherwise, the owls do nothing to the nest, which will hold two or three eggs.

The adult great horned owl stands about two feet tall. Its wingspan is nearly four feet!

Both male and female great horned owls are feathered in a mix of brown, black, and white. Their large eyes are yellow and the "facial disk" around the eyes is red-brown. The tufts of feathers that look like ears or horns—and that give the owl its name—do several things. First, the tufts show the owl's "mood." Also, their different shapes help other owls to know who's who. Last, the tufts are a kind of defense—they make the owl look like a mammal. The owl's real ears are near its eyes, at the edge of the facial disk. And though its ears are not easily seen, the owl's hearing is very good.

The great horned owl's hearing is so good, it can hunt by sound alone!

The female great horned owl is slightly bigger than the male. You cannot tell them apart, though, unless you see them at their nest.

Great horned owls eat almost any small animal they can catch. They'll even kill skunks and porcupines!

COOPER'S HAWK

The Cooper's hawk is built for hunting among trees. Its tail is long, and its wings are short. It can call up quick bursts of speed while weaving in and out of the trees. If a bird or small mammal tries to hide in the tangle of a thorn bush, the hawk may go in on foot to catch it.

Cooper's hawks may mate for life. In early spring, the male picks out a spot for the nest, usually in a pine, hemlock, or spruce tree. The male also does most of the nest building. He builds the nest of layered sticks, and lines it with large pieces of tree bark. The female will lay four or five eggs. The parents will attack a predator that gets too close. During the nesting season, the male does most of the hunting. He brings prey to the nest and gives it to the female. The female will tear up the prey and feed the chicks.

Hawks used to be considered pests because they kill other animals. Today, we know they are important to the balance of nature. The hawk that kills a songbird is not unlike the songbird that kills insects and worms in order to survive. We have given hawks and owls the protection they deserve—it is not legal to kill them anymore.

Young Cooper's hawks are often seen hunting for songbirds at feeders in the winter.

The downy chicks spend more than a month in the nest. Even after they fledge, it will be 30 to 40 more days before they will hunt for themselves.

SNOW AND ICE

makes the perfect home for some birds. Imagine living where a "warm" summer day may see the mercury barely rise above freezing. It may not sound like the perfect place to live, but birds that live near the north and south poles have ways of dealing with these frigid conditions.

Many polar birds grow unusually thick coats of feathers to keep them warm. Some even grow feathers in places where other birds do not. And like the white polar bear and arctic fox, some birds match the snow. The snowy owl stays white all year, but other birds, like the ptarmigan, change their feathers to match the season. Nature has a wonderful way of helping these birds survive long, cold winters.

30

SNOWY OWL

Warm feathers cover everything but the snowy's talons and eyes. They even cover most of its beak.

Most owls are forest birds, but *ookpik* —as the Eskimos call the snowy owl—lives on the tundra, far north of the tree line and any forest. This far north, the frozen ground and biting winds would kill a tree. The snowy owl's hunting perch will be a rock or small hill that gives the owl a view of the area.

Few things escape the snowy's bright yellow eyes. It is watching for tiny movements of small rodents, which make up most of its diet. The white owl eats lemmings, mice, shrews, and voles. If food is hard to find, it will eat arctic hares, ptarmigans, small birds, and even catch fish by wading into water.

Snowy owls are big. They are almost two feet tall, and have a wingspan of about five feet. Females may weigh more than four and one half pounds. They are heavier than great horned owls, which are nearly the same size.

Snowy owls do not migrate. But when the number of lemmings drops, as it does every few years, thousands of snowies go south. They will find more prey in warmer climates. Snowy owls have been seen as far south as Louisiana and Georgia! Snowies will choose places that look like the tundra—open fields, beaches, or airport fields—for their temporary homes.

In the treeless tundra, the snowy owl's nest must be on the ground. The female scrapes a shallow hole in the ground. She will not line the nest, but will simply lay her eggs on the bare earth.

Young snowies hatch in about 33 days, covered with a thick coat of gray down. They keep their coats until they fledge. The parent owls will attack a predator that comes too close to the nest.

PTARMIGANS

The rock ptarmigan and its close relative, the willow ptarmigan, are found in arctic tundras around the world. A third species, the white-tailed ptarmigan, lives high in the Rocky Mountains from Alaska to New Mexico. Ptarmigans are masters of disguise, for they live on the ground. Their nest is nothing more than a small scrape on the ground that is lined with feathers and grass. Living in trees would do them no good, for the trees of the tundra—which is what this land is called—are only a few inches tall!

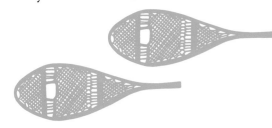

Ptarmigans prefer to walk or run rather than fly. However, if a ptarmigan is in danger, it will take off in a roar of flapping wings that will confuse the enemy. Once it is in the air, the ptarmigan will lock its wings and glide a long way. It will probably land far from where its nest is hidden. If forced to move south for food, ptarmigans will migrate on foot.

When the temperature drops dangerously low, ptarmigans may spend the night under a snow drift. The snow drift will block the winds and actually holds in the bird's body heat. If the ptarmigan simply walked into a drift, an arctic fox or wolf could follow its scent. So instead, the ptarmigan flies—headfirst—into the snow, disappearing in a puff of white!

Ptarmigan chicks are able to move and feed themselves soon after hatching. This way, they are not helpless on the ground if an enemy were to show up.

In the summer, the ptarmigan's feathers are brown. When the days grow shorter, its feathers begin to turn white for winter. For awhile, though, the ptarmigan looks like it has been spattered with white paint.

The ptarmigan wears snowshoes! Feathers on its feet help it to walk on top of the snow.

33

PENGUINS

Like the emperor penguin, king penguin males also hold their eggs on their feet. A special flap of belly skin keeps the egg warm.

These emperor penguin chicks live in a creche, where they are watched by a few adults. This frees both the parents so they can fish for food.

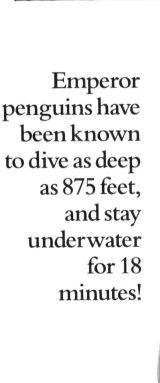

Emperor penguins have been known to dive as deep as 875 feet, and stay underwater for 18 minutes!

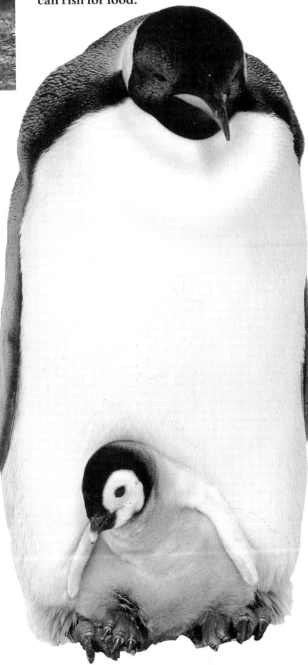

Penguins are not like any other birds in the world. They have completely given up on flight. Instead, they live their lives by—and in—the ocean, where they swim and fish for their food. There are 18 species of penguins, all found in the southern hemisphere. They are not all found in Antarctica, though, as many people think. There are penguins in Australia, New Zealand, Africa, South America, and on many south Atlantic islands. Even though many of these places are far from Antarctica, most have cold ocean currents just off their shores.

The emperor penguin is the largest penguin. It weighs more than 80 pounds and stands almost four feet high. That's almost as tall as a cow! The emperor is found only on the coast of Antarctica, where it nests in huge colonies. Unlike the other penguins, emperor penguins lay their eggs at the beginning of the southern hemisphere winter, when the sun never fully rises and the temperature may drop to –60° Fahrenheit.

The female emperor penguin lays a single egg, but if that egg were to touch the ground, it would instantly freeze. The male emperor penguin stands for six weeks without moving, holding the egg on his feet. A special flap of belly skin covers the egg and keeps it warm. The male eats

Penguin wings have evolved—changed over the years—into strong "flippers" that help them swim.

nothing during this time; he lives off his body fat. When the egg finally hatches, the male leaves the chick in the care of its mother, who has been away all this time, feeding. The male goes off by himself for a well-deserved meal.

The Adélie penguins of Antarctica nest during the South Pole's summer. Millions of these little penguins cover the beaches. Because the weather is a little warmer—reaching 30° Fahrenheit some days—the Adélie can build a crude nest of stones in which to lay their two eggs. The male still does the incubating, though. He sits for seven to eleven days without eating before the chicks hatch and his mate takes charge of them. The Adélie chicks stay in the nest for 22 days. Then they join others their age in a huge creche. With their young in a creche, the parents can both fish for food. Also, there is safety in numbers; the young penguins are less likely to be harmed by an enemy.

To leave the water, a penguin builds up its speed until it can "fly" out of the water and land on its belly or feet!

The little Adélie is the best-known of the penguins.
They adapt well to captivity.

35

FEATHERED JEWELS—

what better way to describe the brightly colored birds of the rain forest? Tropical rain forests are the richest places on

earth—it is no surprise that its birds are the most beautiful on earth.

The toucan, with a bill nearly as long as its body, has a painted clown's face. Parrots chatter from the tops of the lush trees. Honeycreepers, motmots, and hundreds of kinds of hummingbirds join a community of birds with such exotic names as touracos and trogons.

Birds of the rain forest spend much of their time near the tops of the trees in the "canopy." This makes it very difficult to watch and learn about rain-forest birds.

36

TOUCANS

Toucans bark, croak, and squawk. They hardly ever sound like birds!

Toucans are the clowns of the rain forest!

A toucan's bill is so big, you might wonder how the bird holds up its head! A toucan's bill is shaped like a banana and is nearly as long as the bird's body. The beak is really very light, though. It has lots of air spaces inside.

Ornithologists are not sure why toucans have such large, colorful beaks. It may be because fruit often grows on slim branches where the heavy toucan cannot perch. The toucan can sit close to the tree trunk and reach with its bill for food. The bright colors may serve as a warning to other toucans to stay away from a nest. Or, the colors may help attract mates. The colors may help keep a flock together in the dim light of the rain forest, too. There may be a reason we do not yet know.

There are 33 different kinds of toucans. All of them are found in Mexico, Central America, and South America. One of the biggest and most colorful is the keel-billed toucan. The keel-billed toucan is 20 inches long, and its body is mostly black. Its huge bill is green, red, orange, and blue. Most of the other toucans and toucanets—smaller toucans—are brightly colored, too.

The bill of the toucan is lightweight. Its edges are rough like the teeth of a saw.

Toucans are mostly fruit-eaters, though they may use their long bills to reach inside bird nests for eggs or chicks to eat. All toucans will eat insects, lizards, and spiders now and then.

When a toucan swallows fruit, it is doing the fruit tree a service. The fruit may be tasty to the toucan, but inside it is a seed. The seeds pass through the bird and drop to the ground far from the tree on which they grew. The seeds can then sprout into new trees, in a new part of the forest. Not all fruit-eating birds help spread seeds to new places. The stomach juices of the parrot are strong enough to digest seeds.

Toucans usually travel in small flocks. They are always squabbling with each other as they scramble from limb to limb looking for ripe fruit. When birds live together like this, they are called "social birds." Toucans have many calls, and some are loud and unbirdlike. The keel-billed toucan croaks like a small frog. The little emerald toucanet barks like a dog!

Toucans use their long bills to reach fruit growing on narrow branches.

Toucanets are small toucans. They are green with colorful markings.

Many rain-forest birds are becoming endangered because the jungles are being destroyed.

39

RESPLENDENT QUETZAL

When the male quetzal takes off from a branch, he drops off backward. This way he doesn't pull his delicate feathers over a twig.

The feathers of the quetzal are iridescent, meaning that light plays off them in flashes of brilliant colors.

The female quetzal is less brightly colored than her mate. She has none of the long flank feathers, nor does she have a crest. She only has a little red under her tail.

High in the foggy rain-forest mountains of Central America lives the resplendent quetzal. It is one of the most beautiful birds in the world.

The male quetzal is amazing. His body is only the size of a pigeon's, but long, gleaming green flank feathers make him more than two feet long. These flank feathers hide his real tail. His body and chest are bright green with gold. He has a shaggy crest, and his belly is bright red.

The quetzal is found only from southern Mexico to Panama. It lives at least 5,000 feet up the slopes of rugged mountains. The woods that grow here are a special kind of rain forest, known as "cloud forest." It is always raining or foggy in a cloud forest. Every tree branch is covered with orchids, ferns, and other tropical plants. In such a lush place, the quetzal's colors camouflage it well.

Male quetzals use their long flank feathers to attract mates. They sometimes fly in great circles high above the forest, where the females can see them clearly. The mated pair of quetzals look for a rotten tree that is soft, yet still standing. They tear and cut a nest hole in the rotten tree. They may use an old woodpecker hole, and just make it bigger.

COCK-OF-THE-ROCK

The male cock-of-the-rock must be one of the rain forest's strangest-looking birds. It is neon orange in color, and its beak is completely hidden by feathers.

To find a mate, twelve or more males will gather in one spot, which they have cleared of small plants and leaves. Ornithologists call these places "leks." Leks are common among rain-forest birds. Some birds use them year after year.

At the lek, the males wait in the trees for a female to arrive. As soon as she lands, the males begin to crow loudly and fly to the ground. The males stand tall and beat their black and white wings. They try to catch the female's eye. They fly into the trees, then fly down again and beat their wings some more.

Soon, the males stand very still. Their feathers are fluffed up as if they wish to look their best. The female takes her time, and looks closely at each male before she chooses one for her mate.

The female raises the chicks all by herself. She builds the nest and incubates the eggs. She feeds her babies by herself, too. The male does not help. He stays at the lek and tries to attract another mate.

The cock-of-the-rock's neon color helps it attract mates in the gloom of the rain forest.

The cock-of-the-rock seems to have no mouth! Its crest looks like a round helmet when seen from the side. It is as thin as a knife blade from the front.

The female cock-of-the-rock is dark brown, with just a small crest above her bill. She is hard to see among the leaves and shadows.

PARROTS

Parrots are not rain-forest birds only. Some live in hardwood forests, some live in mountains, and some even live at the edge of the desert.

Most parrots live in hollow trees. Many will dig a hole in a termite nest. Others may build nests of twigs or grass.

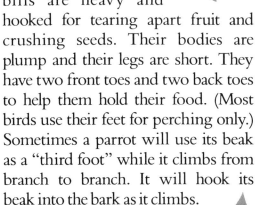

Parrots are found in Central and South America, Africa, Asia, and Australia. No matter where they live, they all have the same basic shape. Their bills are heavy and hooked for tearing apart fruit and crushing seeds. Their bodies are plump and their legs are short. They have two front toes and two back toes to help them hold their food. (Most birds use their feet for perching only.) Sometimes a parrot will use its beak as a "third foot" while it climbs from branch to branch. It will hook its beak into the bark as it climbs.

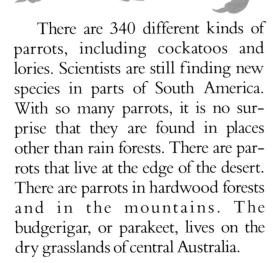

There are 340 different kinds of parrots, including cockatoos and lories. Scientists are still finding new species in parts of South America. With so many parrots, it is no surprise that they are found in places other than rain forests. There are parrots that live at the edge of the desert. There are parrots in hardwood forests and in the mountains. The budgerigar, or parakeet, lives on the dry grasslands of central Australia.

There once was a parrot that lived in the eastern United States. The Carolina parakeet was a beautiful bird, colored green, yellow, and orange. The Carolina parakeet was killed off because it damaged crops; it became extinct in 1920. Another native American species is the thick-billed parrot. It used to be found in the pine forests of Arizona. Thick-billed parrots are being released in the forests again in hopes they will be common once more.

The strangest of the parrots may be the kakapo of New Zealand. This parrot cannot fly; it is nicknamed the "owl parrot." Also from New Zealand is the kea. The kea acts more like a hawk than a parrot. It may even kill sick sheep!

Some parrots are among the most endangered birds in the world. As the rain forests are destroyed, the birds that live there are losing their homes. Many more parrots are taken from their homes in nature and are sold as pets; most are sold in North America. Thousands upon thousands of parrots are captured each year. Many die while being captured or later when transported to stores. To save wild parrots, only those born in captivity should be kept as pets.

Wild parrots live in big, noisy flocks. It can be cruel to keep one parrot in a cage.

Thick-billed parrots like these were once common in the mountains of Arizona. They are being released there to breed and repopulate the forests again.

Macaws are the largest of the parrots. This green-winged macaw will grow to be 35 inches from bill to tail.

Adaptations (ad-ap-TAY-shuns): Changes that happen over a long time—maybe millions of years—that help an animal or plant survive.

Brood: A family of baby birds.

Cache (kash): To store or hide food for later use.

Camouflage (KAM-oh-flahj): Colors that help an animal hide in nature.

Clutch (kluch): A complete set of eggs. Some birds lay more than one clutch each year.

Colony: A group of birds that nest close to each other.

Courtship: The act of attracting a mate. A bird may sing, share food, or show off its feathers when courting.

Creche (kresh): A large group of baby birds who are, like in a nursery, watched by a few adults.

Crest: A pointy tuft of feathers on the head of a bird.

Crop: A pouch in a bird's throat where food is stored after it is swallowed, but before it goes to the stomach.

Endangered species: A kind of animal or plant that is so rare it may become extinct.

Environment: All parts of the surroundings—air, water, land, weather, plants, and animals—and the way they all act together.

Extinct: A species that is no longer living, like the dinosaur and passenger pigeon.

Fledge (fledj): To leave the nest for the first time. A "fledgling" is a young bird that has just left the nest.

Flock: A group of birds that stay together for protection or to find food.

Habitat (HAB-uh-tat): Where an animal lives; the special kind of environment it needs to survive.

Incubate (IN-kyoo-bayt): To keep eggs warm so they will hatch. An incubating bird sits on the eggs, warming them with its body heat.

Lek (lek): A place where many male birds gather, in hopes of attracting a female.

Mate: To breed; some birds mate for life, others may stay together only until the eggs are laid.

Migrate (MEYE-grayt): To move from one area to another, usually over long distances. Many birds migrate south to escape cold winters, and migrate north again in the spring.

Molt: To replace old feathers with new ones.

Nestling (NEST-ling): A chick, from the time it hatches to the time it leaves the nest.

Ornithologist (or-ni-THAHL-oh-jist): A scientist who studies birds.

Plumage (PLOO-muj): A bird's feathers.

Predator (PRED-uh-tor): Any animal—including birds—that catches, kills, and eats other animals.

Prey (pray): The animals that are eaten by predators. For example, songbirds are the usual prey of Cooper's hawks.

Range: The area over which a kind of bird is found.

Roost: The place where a bird spends the night; a "roost hole" is a hole where a bird spends the night, or where it takes shelter in bad weather.

Scavenger (SKAV-en-jer): An animal or bird that feeds on dead or discarded things, rather than catching live prey.

Species (SPEE-shees): A group of closely related living things that are much alike and that can breed with one another in the wild.

Suet (SOO-et): Hard, uncooked beef fat. Many birds will eat suet.

Territory (TEHR-ri-tor-ee): The area a bird—or pair of birds—defends as theirs. Some birds will even defend their territory against other birds of their species.

Wingspan: The distance from one wing tip to the other, when a bird has its wings fully spread.